No Tall Buildings in Nazareth

No Tall Buildings in Nazareth

Parent-child conversations on religion
By Tom Johnson

Drawings by Dan Marshall

HARPER & ROW, PUBLISHERS

New York, Evanston, San Francisco, London

FIRST EDITION

Designed by Dan Marshall and Lydia Link

Library of Congress Cataloging in Publication Data

Johnson, Tom, 1923–
  No tall buildings in Nazareth.
  1. Religious education of children.
I. Title.
BV1475.2.J56   201'.1   72–160640
ISBN 0–06–064193–2

To Sarah, Denise and Tom.
I blame them each for this.
And a special thanks to Natalie.

Introduction

When I wrote this I wanted a child's book. One the child can stay with. A look at the basics of his or her religion and some thoughts on Christian life.

Friends say I have failed. That, if anything, the book is more for themselves than for children they have known. Maybe they are right; if so, it's not surprising. Failing our children is a commonplace.

But think of the book as trying to help the child through the parent. It tries to find answers both of them can live with, maybe even enjoy, and won't have to put aside as soon as the child becomes a little older. The parent can use the book as a guide—read it, keep whatever appeals and lie in wait for the child. If the child is ten through twelve or so, the parent can be spared; the child can read the book himself.

Like children, the book does have questions plus some answers I have hope for. I hope they suggest a common reach we would like our children to have.

To Start With

To Start With

Did God create the world?

This always sounds like an overstatement. But yes. Something very big to say.

How did he do it?

Probably in the wonderful way that science tells about. Where a great cloud formed in an orbit around the sun and, having the right parts and a good temperature, settled and sorted itself very slowly into land, and water, and air. And while this was happening, small and promising forms of life took hold, and changed over millions of years into all the trees, and all the grass, and all the other plants we find. And all the lower animals, and man.

Does everybody believe in God?

No. Big parts of the world and many of those around us don't, including your Aunt Natalie. And none of the lower animals do.

Why doesn't everyone believe in God?

There are many reasons. Maybe man has many things to learn about himself, and many things to learn about his world, and many things to do for his fellow man before he can offer himself to his God.

Besides, if everyone believed in God, too many of our Einsteins might be monks instead. And who would tell us how worlds are made?

What's an Einstein?

A scientist. A smart one. The one we hear about believed, but some of his partners don't. People see with different eyes.

Why does anyone believe in God?

There are many reasons. Most do because their parents teach them. Or simply because it seems more right than wrong. Then if they are lucky, they grow to love the idea of God. And if they are very lucky, they grow to love God himself.

Besides, if nobody believed in God, Saint Francis might have been a huntsman, and walked through the woods with a rifle in his hands shooting squirrels from their perch.

What did Saint Francis really do?

According to the story, the animals of the forest would gather around him, and were friends with him, and completely unafraid. But a thing to remember about Saint Francis is that he seemed very pleased with God's world. And he taught us that all things in life are special. And not just the peacock. And not just you.

This is a special world then?

This is Earth. We were born from her and we live with her. She is truly our mother and we must honor her. We must see that her air is clean, her waters good to be in, her fields green. And we must see that all her animals, even her ugly ones, have little reason to run from us. And while we're about it, we should do our best to feed each and every one of her people.

God wants these things?

No question about it. And your Aunt Natalie agrees.

All The Crazy Christians

What does Christian mean?

Christian is a way of life. A way to spend our days and thirty of our years, or ninety-nine. One who believes in God and says that God is with us now. One who believes that Christ was God, that Christ was God and man. That being man is important. That being man is good. That each of us is good. Has goodness in our heart, has seeds of goodness in our heart.

That the world can be good. That the world can be better if more of us will try. That God insists we try and God will help us as we try.

One who loves his friends indeed and even those who aren't his friends.

How many Christians are there?

About 42.

Is that all?

No. Not if we start counting and close our eyes a bit. For we have to count them all. Everyone who calls himself a Christian. Everyone who hopes he is. Everyone who tries.

And if we go ahead and count we can reach our way to five or six or seven hundred million, and maybe even more, and we can count ourselves.

For each of us has things to do. Things that Christian people do. Things that are hard and sometimes not, things that are easy and fun. Reaching for someone who needs our help, listening now for a friend.

Then a Christian is the same as everyone else?

A little more fun to watch. A little strange to see.

He looks at his world and he does its work, but, strangely enough, he prays. In church for awhile or brushing his teeth, a Christian begins to pray.

Yes, a Christian begins to pray, saying that God is here. Helping us listen when someone calls, helping us listen and see. Helping us see our world. Helping us do its work.

Yes, the God we want is at work. Here in his usual way. Working in our hearts and in the shadows of our mind. Here in his usual way.

Spirit

God is here?

The Holy Spirit is here. The Spirit we call God. The Spirit with us now. God who enters our lives to help us. God at our elbow. God who is pleased to dine with us.

The one that Christ has sent. To help us change our world. To help discover truth and make the people glad.

God working with his people. The Spirit in the world. The Goodness in the land.

The Goodness in what land?

This earth of ours. Where all of us live, or maybe you have other plans.

Does the Bible tell about the Spirit?

Yes. In many ways. People in the Bible did extraordinary things, very good and very bad and somewhere in between. Those who did the better thing were working with the Spirit. He helped them in their work.

That is what we think of him. Good to have around. He helps to get things done. It's important to remember the Bible is a special book. It tells about the things of man and that, alone, is good. It tells the word of God, which makes it even better. It says that neither is alone, that God and man are working here together, which makes it best of all.

The Holy Spirit appeared when Christ himself was baptized. It says in the Bible the baptism was done by John, a man called John the Baptist, a man who talked of Christ before the others knew him.

When the baptism was finished, the voice of God was heard and the Spirit of God was seen. The voice said Christ was the Son of God, that God was pleased with him, and the Spirit was seen as a dove. A single dove, there with Christ, the Spirit there with Christ. The Father and the Son and the Spirit with the Son. The Spirit with us now.

Why was the Spirit a dove?

Instead of a crow? Crows are much too noisy. The Spirit works in quiet ways.

A Little More on Prayer

Is it really strange to pray? You said it was.

Perhaps it is. But strange in a nice kind of way.

Everything around us has many things to do. Everything that walks or flies or swims, or moves from here to there for reasons of its own. They all have work to do. They have work to do and time enough to play. They eat and sleep and work and play, and many have young to care for. They live and feel pleasure. They have life enough. They live.

But man is somehow different. He works and plays like all the rest. He eats and sleeps and cares for his young. But man is somehow strange. He has life enough and pleasure, but still he looks for more. He looks for other things to do.

So he colors and shapes and builds to the sky. He colors and shapes and makes things grow and he makes his own music and sings. He reads the simplest book. He reads the hardest book. Man is reaching out and doing.

That's how man is different. That's how man is strange. He reaches out for more. He has life enough and pleasure, but he looks around for more. So he calls for a poem and he calls for a song and he reaches for God and he prays.

Yes, prayer is good and prayer is strange. As different,

as strange as man. As different, as strange as us.

Aunt Natalie. Is she strange, too?

She has her little ways and worries us a little but we never run away. We know she is a blessing in a very good disguise.

God and Man

When we reach for God, how do we know?

We can tell from our thoughts and by watching our hands.

When we think of man—of you and me and everyone else—we sometimes think of God. When we think of man we are starting to reach and we sometimes think of God.

But God plays games with us. He lets us think of him and then he turns our thoughts around and makes us think of man again. He makes us think of people. Their music, their books, the things they want, and all of the friends they need.

That's one of the ways we reach for God. When our thoughts are reaching out. When our thoughts reach out to man.

But what about our hands?

Our hands go out to one another. To help and comfort and touch. For man is the closest one we have. The

God and Man

different and special and closest one. The closest one to God.

But what if we're alone, with no one else around?

It really doesn't matter, nothing here is changed. Even all alone, we are still a part of man. We share in his joy and his spirit and we know and we feel his pain.

And we look for God where everyone looks. We look for God in our hearts and minds, and we reach for man in our prayers. In the shapes and colors and books he makes, in our thoughts and in our prayers.

Some of us want it that way. Some of us choose to be alone.

A Capuchin is alone. A Capuchin is a monk. He lives with other people but most of his life is alone. He lives with other people but most of his life is a prayer. God must like his prayers. He lets him pray for many things. He lets him pray for us.

We are each a part of man. None of us walks away. Even when we're alone, we are always a part of man.

Which part are we?

Whichever we decide. The twinkle in his eye or the water on his knee.

What does it really mean, to be a part of man?

It means we're all together. The world is ours to make and there are many things we want.

If it's truth we want, we stand with those who try it, all of those who listen, all of those who look. If it's jus-

11

tice, we ask for those who seek it and we search with them awhile.

If it's love we want, we love. If it's God, we honor him. If it's darkness, we have ways. Turn our backs on truth —the light will go away. Live and never love.

The world is what we make it and it waits for you and me.

A Problem

What if someone hits me? Is it right to hit him back?

Not below the belt. Never below the belt.

Did Christ say that?

No. The Marquis of Queensbury did.

Christ suggested we look in our hearts. We might find a sadness there. The sadness of striking at someone. The wish that it wouldn't be done.

It's right to feel the sadness. It's best not to hit at all. When we fight, our world goes wrong for a while and we wonder at what we've done.

We are much too old to fight. If we wonder, even a little, we are much too old to fight.

So, we shouldn't be hitting each other. Above the belt or below. Above the belt and, as Queensbury said, certainly not below.

What if he hits me again? Right in the mouth and it hurts?

What will be, will be.

Those Around Us

When I walk around the world, do I love all the people I see?

Probably not, but maybe we should. People look better that way. People we love are always good to see.

Too often we forget. It isn't always easy to see how close we are, how very much the same. Each of us is different and isn't it delightful and other times it's not, but we are very much the same.

For much of what we want is all alike. Someone here to honor us. People here to be with. Be with and work with and talk. Work with and play with and laugh. People to cry with awhile.

Christ said we should love them. He said it's important we do. He said that we should and some of us can. It's a little like loving ourselves.

The problem now for most of us is proving Christ was right, to show his words are true. That we can love ourselves and love the others too. It isn't always easy but we're wiser if we do.

Can't we love others without knowing Christ?

Yes, but some of us find him useful.

For Christ is a way of looking at man. A way of looking at man to see what man can be. Finding man at peace. At peace with himself, at peace with the world, at home with the world and all of its life, at peace with those in need.

For Christ is the beautiful one. A way of looking at man when we find it hard to see. Christ, indeed, is the beautiful one. The things that we can be. Christ, for you and me, is the things that we can be.

Even me? Could I be like Christ?

Even you.

Aunt Natalie, too?

Even her. Always doing what he asked and never understanding how close she is to him and him to her. She's a little slow that way.

Sand and Soul and Silliness Too

Christians do some funny things. Like giving things up without a real reason. Aren't we silly sometimes?

Yes, but it keeps the soul in shape. The part of us that God wants. The soul we take along when we walk our favorite path and listen for the earth. When we listen for the sea and walk along the sand.

My soul is here with me right now. Somewhere deep within. Innermost, I think, is where my soul begins. My soul is only me; my soul is me, inside.

Everybody has one, partly seen and partly known. Seen in what we do. Heard in our music and found in our books, there in the best of both. Known by what we have or what we hope for and keeping certain secrets to itself.

Giving things up and doing without helps the soul to grow. It lets us reach around, choosing anyone we please and telling God we care. We offer this for them. If we like, we choose ourselves, anyone in need of things, anyone will do.

It lets the soul grow deeper when we learn to do without and wider in its reach. We share with those who suffer if we will suffer too, just by giving something up, if now and then we do.

The Color of God

Is God the same color as me?

No. God is a very bright orange.

That's true?

No. But God is colorful indeed. As colorful as truth. As colorful as peace. As colorful as love.

Never only white and never only black. Never only yellow, red or brown. God looks more like you and me each time we look for peace. God looks more like each of us each time that we have loved.

What does that mean?

That each of us is close to God.

Close in what we think, not the colors that we wear. Close in what we do. By the markings of our soul, not our wisdom or our ways or any color in our eyes or on our hands.

For each of us is man and what we think will either join us or keep us far apart, and everything we do will decide how close we are.

So let our people live. It's easier that way. To be with one another, me with you or you with me, or whatever way there is to help us know each other more.

So come and see a friend. Or come a little closer so a friend can come to you.

Which always pleases God. For God enjoys our many colors when we enjoy them too.

How do you know God isn't orange?

Because God is a favorite of mine and orange is not my favorite color.

Something to Remember

What should Christians remember the most?

Remember always God. The fondest wish, the only wish. The wish we see in every wish. God is what we want.

God is what we miss. God to come, God to stay, God for us to be with, God for us to know. God, we want to know you.

It's important to remember him. Remember him right now and remember him again. Remember him the most when joy and gladness pass, when sadness comes and things need looking after.

That sounds sad.

Yes and no. We have sadness, we have joy. Most of us have both. There are moments with our God, moments with ourselves, and many long hours with man. Man like you. Man like me. Those who need each other now. Those who need each other most when joy and gladness pass and things need looking after.

If God is what we miss, how do we ever find him?

Look a little harder and reach a little more. Look around for truth and find him looking too. Reach around for peace and reach for him.

Something to Remember

Do anything we please, do a holy, godly thing, go to someone now, be gentle with a friend. Touch a friend and feel his touch. Know your God is there.

The God we want will come. He doesn't like to stay away.

Does Aunt Natalie ever pray?

To God? He hasn't heard from her in years. Not everyone's so lucky.

Are Christians mostly happy?

Only when their God is pleased and never when he's sad. Yes if they do his work and no if they turn away, and never when your stomach hurts or somewhere just as bad.

Yes if they feel that man is good. No if they feel he's mostly bad and no if they only laugh at him and make him smaller now.

Yes if they feel that God and man have things to do together, and no if they feel that God is much too far away.

Never when we hide ourselves and keep ourselves away, and never when your stomach hurts again.

Sometimes we are happy and sometimes we are not, but we stand a better chance when we remember Christ was God and Christ was also man. That Christ was one of us. Different in his special way, yet man like each of us.

Is Aunt Natalie happy?

Her analyst won't say. It's a secret with the two of them, her analyst and her. We will pray she is.

What's an analyst?

One more person trying to help another. Trying to make her feel good. Telling her she's lucky she isn't more like me.

Does Aunt Natalie want to be like you?

Anything but that. Anything is better than a Christian she would say. Our holiness is hollow and our heads are filled with prayers.

Is she right?

Prayers are mostly from the heart. But each of us should answer that ourselves. We can make her right or wrong.

Men and Women, Boys and Girls

Why do we always talk about man? Why not ever woman? Isn't woman as good as man?

We thought you'd never ask.

Man is all of us at once. Man is each of us and everyone. Men and women and children. The young and the very old. Everyone is man.

It's a little like speaking of God. We don't always mean what we say. We call him he and him and father, but God is always more. God is always something different. God is always more.

Some of the women call him she. They call him she and her and mother, words they like, words that bring him close. They call him she and mother, which makes the children laugh and sing and troubles all the men.

But God is always more. Saying he or saying she, God is always more. Saying her or saying him.

More than father, more than mother, God is always something different, something better, something more.

So it is with man. Man is more than you and me and more than her and him. Man is everybody here and all the world is his, or maybe hers.

Why are boys and girls different?

So children can be born, so children can be loved. We want a mother and a father, but that is only part. There are other reasons too. The differences will bring us close. Fill us full of wonder and bring us very close.

The differences are good. The differences are fun. Boys and girls are different. Boys and girls are fun.

To learn a different love, grow a little older, learn a different, better love. To love someone who isn't like ourselves. Where loving someone different is a special kind of love.

The differences are there. The differences are good. They bring a special love.

21

You didn't mention God.

The differences of God. They also bring a special love. Fill us full of wonder and bring a special love.

Goodness

If the differences are good, what is goodness anyway? When is something good?

Everything that helps is what we mean by good.

If I am free and you are free, it's good. If you help me and I help you, it's good.

If I like you and you like someone else, both of us are good. But if and when you like me, too, you are really good.

And Freedom

What is being free?

Doing what we please. No matter if it's right, no matter if it's wrong and that's not right at all.

Being free is having freedom and freedom is a trust I have, a trust I give to you. A trust that someone gave to me and I will give to you. You will break it now and then, but what it means is that you do the things you want, you do the things you please except you bring no harm. You do not harm another and you will not harm

Goodness

yourself or break the better rules. You do the things you want, and all of us will hope that what you want is good.

A trust we have in people, a trust we give ourselves, that most of what we want is good and often even best.

That we are happiest when free and always look our best when we choose the better thing, when we are free to make a choice and choose the better thing. People have a right to look their best. People have a right to make the choice.

People all together. As a family, as a city, as a country, as a world. We like to have the people working all together, free to choose the rules they want, free to choose the one that's right and change the one that's not.

Is freedom hard or easy?

Always a little of both. It hurts a little to give a freedom up, but once in a while we do. A freedom goes away.

A freedom I enjoy might be hurting someone else so he and I must look around and find a better one. One that doesn't hurt as much, or doesn't hurt at all. We hope it helps instead. Any good and happy Christian wants the same. A freedom goes away but, if things are working right, a better one has come.

Freedom has its limits, freedom has its rules. God has rules too. Our conscience lets us know and we should try to understand his rules. They help us live together. They tell us to be honest, they tell us to be fair. They tell us we are good and to let the goodness show.

For goodness is the thing that counts. Goodness is the seed. The seed that brings us freedom, the faith I have in you, the faith you have in me, the trust we have in man.

I think that even you are good. I hope it doesn't scare you. I hope that you have freedom too. I hope you always will.

Parents and Someone to Honor

Do we have to honor our parents?

Yes, we should always honor our parents. They might need it very badly. And we should honor all the children. They will need it badly too.

Is Aunt Natalie a parent?

Very much a parent. She looks for children everywhere and tells them what to do. What she doesn't say to them, she says to me.

How do we honor someone?

There are many different ways. An easy way is just to say hello. To recognize. To say hello. Letting someone know he's really not alone. If he really doesn't want to be, he's really not alone.

Seeing everyone around us as an equal part of man. No more than any one of us and certainly not less. Having different color and having different ways, richer now and poorer, calling other places home, brighter than the rest of us and maybe not so bright, someone near and someone far, our father and our mother or someone we don't know, seeing each of us as man and very close for that.

In spite of different ways we are brothers, we are sisters, and we honor one another just in recognizing that.

But don't we honor some a little more? Aren't some people better and different?

Thank God for special people. They brighten up our world, they brighten up our days. Someone close or someone gifted. One who tries to understand. All the ones who help. And we honor them in special ways. We seek them out, we need them. What they are we often like, what they bring us often helps. The ones we like the best. We pray that everybody has one. Everyone around us needs someone rather special to brighten up his world.

Is Aunt Natalie special?

If a hundred people met her, ninety-nine would say she was and the one that's left is the only one that's wrong.

I don't think I like him.

Who?

The one that likes to hit me. The one we talked about.

Stay away from him. Avoid him like the plague. Find a horse or find a trolley and ride away from him.

Everyone and Us

All we talk about is others. What about ourselves?
Don't we ever think of us?

Now and then we do, we think about ourselves. Any
time and any place. We have much to think about and
many questions too.

Am I close to anyone, am I close enough to God? Am
I reaching out for something? Do I reach for something
good?

What are the things to build, what are the things to
grow, what are the things to do? And what about this
earth? If the earth is troubled and darker, do we look for
other ways? Do we look for promising workable ways,
where the world can be and we can be and man can have
his things. A place to care for the young, a place for
children to learn and play, a place for the young and
old?

We have much to think about. Is it good to be a child
of God, to be a part of man, sharing in the joy and
sharing in the pain? To know that peace is sometimes
sadness, that someone needs us now?

For people are looking around, and someone needs us
now to brighten up his world. To share with him and
brighten things and tell him someone cares. Needing
someone close. One that he will like. Someone very special. Someone here like us.

I have many things to learn and many things to love, so what is a child and what is a word and where is a child for me?

But what if we don't care? What if we only think of ourselves and not the other things? What if we just don't care?

Then a Capuchin will pray. It's best that we be careful for a Capuchin will pray. He will pray for you and the rest of us, that none of us gets away.

Praying that God will come to one of us. That things will start to happen and things that should will be, sooner or later will be. That things will start to happen and some of us will help, thinking of things that we must do and doing things we must.

What if we still don't care?

Chances are we won't. Chances are good we still won't care. Not all of us are lucky, not all of us will help.

That's one of the reasons we multiplied. We filled the earth with people so God would have a chance. A chance to find some more, a few of his people more who are willing to do his work.

And God has ways to find them. God has ways and means and now and then we know. A man somewhere discovers a truth and a child looks up and is glad, a woman discovers her world and the child is glad again. Some of the things will happen, some of the things will be.

God has many ways. Insistent ways, and strange, and sometimes very slow, slower when we hide ourselves and keep ourselves away.

How does a woman discover a world?

The same way a man does. She looks inside herself to see what God has given her and what she finds inside of her that all the world should see. What she would like to do, especially for you, especially for me.

God Gets All The Credit

If we're the ones that do the work, why do we say "thank God"?

It's our way of being modest. Closer to the truth, it's our way of being humble, being honest with ourselves.

Thanking God for what his people are. Thanking him that some of them have cared. And thanking him for all the times when something I did wrong turned out right instead.

Maybe that's when he is best. Maybe every time I fail it only hurries him and speeds him up and something here gets done a little faster. God make that be true!

If God is around, why do we worry about things?

God is with us now but so are the wars we fight. The threat of war, the horror of war, the threat and often the fact. God is with us now but so is a troubled earth. The land, the water, the air. The earth that gives us life, the earth that threatens now.

God is here and the cities cry, the cities cry in pain, in squalor, dirt and pain. God is with the poor and their voice is seldom heard. God is with us now but the pain is very clear.

Man has fear of man, fear and scorn have crowded him, with little room for hope, with little room for grace. The help that comes when God and man have things to do together.

Pain was there with Christ and pain is with us here. The problems and the pain. Problems we must solve.

A little more room is what we need, so push aside the fear, we say, push aside the scorn, a little more room for God. Problems to solve with our hearts and our minds, with the help of God, with grace, with our hands and hearts and minds, and the way the earth is turning, not without the pain.

Aunt Natalie says the best thing we can do for God is just forget him.

She's right if all we ever do is pray and go to church. If all of us just sit and wait and look around to see what God has done.

God is here to help, but the work is yours and mine. He might be waiting now to see what one of us will do.

He will listen to our prayers, but what he likes best is to help us with our work.

Does God only work with somebody good?

He picks and chooses from all of us, regardless of who we are, and whether we know him or not, slightly good or slightly bad and maybe surprising to see.

Choosing those most likely or those who seem most strange, who do his work in common ways or do the strangest things, ways that we're accustomed to or ways that worry us at times. Any one of us will do.

For the good we do is shared. If God finds good in one of us, God finds good in man. Something he can recognize and work with. Something here that calls. Choosing whom he will, one who seems quite likely or one who seems quite strange, anyone will do. One like those around us or someone strange like you.

Us Again

It's nice of speak of man and all, but what about ourselves again?

The best of what there is was surely meant for us. The happiest thought is privately mine. The truly joyous thing occurs with me around.

The fairy tales were written for me. Mine are the

things to do, mine is the meaning of things. The best of all the poems speaks quietly of me.

The time we give ourselves is special time indeed. When the world is ours alone.

No limits on my nonsense, no limits on my truth. When foolishness is fun and thinking has no fear, when all the thoughts are mine and I'm the only one I hear, when I am here alone, when I am here with me.

Yes, the time we give ourselves is always special time. It gives us hope and gives us courage when we speak of man again. Knowing he has thoughts like ours and foolish moments too. That he is one like us. That on his better days he holds the world close and knows his favorite poem was truly meant for him.

Is that something good or something bad?

Something very good. To hold the world close. To be a part of things. To be and understand. With all our truth and all our nonsense, to be and understand. To think about our world. The millions and millions of people, the hundreds and billions of stars and even all the crawly things.

How good and different God must be that things should be this way. That the happiest thought, with all of this, is somehow yours and mine, that the best of all the poems speaks of us.

That everyone can feel this way. All the rest and you. All the rest and me.

Is she very smart?

Aunt Natalie? Very smart and very clever too. God will say the same. He hasn't caught her yet and he's been chasing her for years.

Someone Stays Behind

Are Christians the best people?

Some of us are and some of us aren't. Yes and often no.

See who has the suffering. See who has the pain. They have a way of seeming best. Those who suffer most and all of those who care.

The tired, the sick, the poor. The lonely and the slow. They make us feel we only pretend, that our days are make-believe. Pretending at our troubles, at worry over games.

Pretending with our problems and worrying with games, for the poor have all the hunger now and seven times the pain.

The tired and the poor. The lonely and the slow. These and all the rest. All of us seem to know.

Should all of us be poor then?

No. And here we go again.

Here we go with the colors we like and the music and

books again. Here we go with our friends. Whatever helps us grow.

For life is a matter of growing. That's what we should do. Reaching up and all around, asking everyone along. Careful with our step and asking everyone along.

But the poor will stay behind. They have other things to do. To spend their time with hunger, to spend their time with pain and making us unsure.

Unsure with our beautiful colors and shapes. Unsure with our books and our friends. Knowing someone stays behind. Seeing someone there.

Why don't we just make everybody richer?

There are many different reasons. For one, it's very hard and maybe God has failed. Christ has failed, the Spirit has failed, the spirit of man is slow.

God has failed to catch us. He fails to catch our ear. Calling with people in need of things, but few of us will hear.

He tells of people needing things. Open and honest and everywhere things. As simple as something to eat. As simple as something to wear. A place to care for the young.

Maybe we should listen. Maybe we should hear. Call a hundred soldiers home and put away our fear.

Call a hundred soldiers and tell them what we know. To put aside the things of war, to put aside the sinister things, the costly and secret and sinister things, that the people are asking for different things, as simple as something to eat, as simple as something to wear, a place to care for the young.

Can we do that?

Maybe we can do it now by halves. We do many things by halves. Keeping half our soldiers now.

Only half of our sinister things. Something we could try.

The problem is the world itself, the world is in our way. We must solve her many problems and put aside her wars. Use her wealth in other ways. Use it on her people and see what we can do. A wish for each of us.

Would Aunt Natalie like that too?

She says we couldn't do it, we would spoil it with a prayer. Cut your prayers in half, she'd say, we do many things by halves.

Does God really fail us like you said?

No. It's the other way around. We often fail him. We overlook a helper, we overlook a friend.

We grow accustomed now. We are used to what we have and used to what we do. Doing something once, doing something twice. We have our way of doing things and, being careful now, we can keep on doing things in the very same old way. It is easy, even good sometimes, to keep on doing things in much the same old way.

But the poor have waited long. Our thoughts are tired and our ways are old and the poor have waited long. We have need for difference here. The difference in getting things done. The differences of God.

God the different. God the best. Always what we want

and never what we are. Always what we wish for and always what we need.

And he works in his different and usual way. Here in our hearts and minds. With the seed of human goodness, with a heart that looks for change.

When he comes and we are willing, when he finds somebody here, when one of us will listen and one of us will see. When our thoughts are tired and our ways are old and the poor have waited long.

Is Aunt Natalie poor?

Her husband says she's working at it, working very hard. He thinks she might succeed.

Things We Like

How do we know when things are good? Things we have around us?

It makes us glad with one another and happy with ourselves when things that are with us are good.

We can tell when things are good. They tend to bring us close. Close to the world we live in, close to the world that God has made, close to the world of man. Whatever teaches or reminds us the world is worth our time.

The colors, the music, the books. And even all the dogs and all the flowers too, and all the better songs and the dances people do.

And we like the people who feel the same. Those who

think the world is good enough to share and treasure everything around that tells them this is so. Those who want the same for others and look for better ways. Who want the same for others and search for better ways.

How about candy and things like that? Are they good to have around?

Only if there's some for me.

What about Godthings?

We need those too. To remind us God is near, the Spirit of God is near.

Quiet things in quiet ways or clearly happy and joyous things. Telling us again that our joy is a promise of things to come, to share it now with friends. That our pain is not for long.

Reminding us to try. That the work of man is the work of God, for man is indeed a child of God. So clear a space for man right now and save a place for God.

Do we have to believe in God? Can't we be happy without him?

It depends on what we think of man. Happiness comes close when we learn to honor man. When we learn to honor people.

The way that God has made it. To know and honor man. For man comes first, we know him first and knowing God comes later, as a child knows its mother, only later knows itself.

To know and honor man. There is happiness in that.

In truth, in love, in all the things he looks for, in all the things of God.

We can stay away from God, be happy just with man. We can walk away from God but not the things of God. Man has need for things like that.

I wish he'd go away.

Who? God?

No, the hitter in my life. The one that likes to hit me.

Find a friend that he's afraid of. Learn to love your friend. Keep him very close.

The Wanted and the One

Why are the good things always God's?

That's what God is all about. God is what there is. All the good together, all the good at once, all the good is God.

The truth we want is God, a hundred times the truth. The love we need is God, a hundred times the love. The justice people seek, a hundred times again. God is these, and beauty. God is these, and peace.

God is each of these. If we look for any one of them, we surely look for him. God is what there is. The Bringer of Things, The Doer, the Wanted and the One. Good things start with him.

Beauty Is For Us

What is beauty?

Something I have seen. Something seen or touched or heard, when something in me knows. I always call it beauty when something I have found becomes a part of me. When I have met with something good. When I like what I have seen. I will gladly take it now, I will come for it again.

Beauty is for us. I see it there for you, I see it there for me. What is beautiful I want, I am glad that it is there and I will look for it once more. We will go and look together.

We will see if it has silence, we will see if it has joy, we will see what he has kept for us today.

I know all that. What's love?

Love is the willingness we have to share ourselves with others. Wanting someone near, liking people, liking life. We always call it love when there are moments in our heart for those who come our way. When we see and understand. When we see that we are close.

Love is for the both of us. Myself and those I love, I am better when I do and so are you.

Someone calls and we will listen. We will listen with our hearts, we will listen with our minds and we know

Beauty Is For Us

that all our listening is one more way we love.

I know that, too. What's justice?

Something we have needed. We seek it out for others and we want it for ourselves.

The world is yours to share. Yours to like and give to me and share with someone else. We always call it love when people want to share, we always call it justice when they do.

When we find the one who waits, the one who waits for you. The one who waits for me.

Justice is for all of us. It follows after love. It will come if we will let it. It will come if we will love.

I know about truth, too. But what is it anyway?

Truth is what we need to understand our world. To know the many different ways we can help each other now. We always call it truth when we speak of what there is to know, what man has known, what man must learn, what some of us will look for, what some of us will find. We are glad for those who look. We are glad for those who let them look, we like the ones who help.

Truth has many reasons. It is something we can love. It has a beauty of its own.

It is something we should have when it is justice that we seek.

What's peace? When someone isn't hitting you?

Peace is being closer. Close to love and close to beauty. Close to justice, close to truth.

If not exactly truth, at least the feeling I am closer and I like the way it feels. If not exactly justice, if not exactly beauty, if not completely love, at least the feeling they will come and the quiet they will bring.

We always call it peace when things are what they are and we are pleased that it is so. When God is in his heaven and God is with us now. When the world is looking better than it did an hour ago, or any day this week. The quiet in my soul.

Peace is better than the other way. The opposite of peace is when we start to feel anxious and hardly pleased at all. Even worse than that, the opposite of peace is often struggle, often war.

We can see that peace is good. We like to have it come, we like to have it stay, and we worry with the others each time it gets away.

More Sand

Which of those things is best? Truth or love or what?

Justice, of course! Justice is having a little of each.

For truth is the sunlight and peace is the dew and beauty is all of the flowers in reach. And love? Love is like running in white summer sand, but justice, sweet justice, is having them each.

I won't ask that again.

Please don't.

Things to Do and Voices to Hear

Of all the things we do, which ones are God's work?

Everything that helps. Caring for the young. Caring for the old. Taking care of me.

When we build a proper bridge. When we build a proper building. When we build a proper home.

The study of man and his world. Our ways of learning and finding out and the study and telling of God.

Read a book or write a play, throw a discus, help a child.

The ways of man when he tries. People with things to do. At work in our fields, at work in our shops. All the things that help.

Every act of thoughtfulness. Every act of love.

Does Aunt Natalie do any of this?

Most of it, yes. And everything she does, she does the best. Nothing holds her back or frightens her away. She hasn't built a bridge or put a building up, but that's an oversight we're sure.

Is there more for us to do?

More than one of us can handle. We need a little help.

Care for the earth that keeps us, feeds us all and keeps us. Care for her well, for the earth is troubled deeply. We have bothered her but good.

Take a look and see. The waters are troubled, the air is not clean, we have littered her pathways well. The earth that God has given we have darkened for a while.

And it seems the earth is calling, saying other things as well. Saying God has numbered his people and the earth is quickly full, and where in the world will we put them unless our children are few.

Children that we love. That our children should be few.

It's always a matter of life. Of land enough and water enough and fuel enough and food. A matter of life and how we live, how our children's children live. Some of us are sure of this and some are not so sure. But it seems the earth is saying we have things to think about.

The joy of giving life. The joy and the goodness of giving life. The joy and the question too.

Why listen to the earth? What about God?

How else could God be talking. How else can God be heard, except in the sounds of the earth, except in the voices of man.

It's important to remember Christ, important that he was God, important that he was man. For God had things to say and he used the voice of man. He used the body and the voice and the things he used he was. Christ was truly man.

God still has things to say and he says them everyday.

44

Not as clearly God, not with us quite like Christ, but the Spirit of God at work.

We look too far for him. We should learn to look around when someone looks for truth, when someone looks for justice, when someone looks for peace. We should learn to look around and listen for our God.

Listen very carefully. We might hear sacred things. The Spirit of God at work. The Spirit with his people, heard on the voices of man.

How do we know who says what's right and hear the things we should?

We look around again. We listen for the truth. We listen with a question and a taste for what is good. God knows we have a question, pray God our taste is good.

We have the Scriptures too—the writings in the Bible —the other words of God. God who is the Father and the ways and words of Christ.

And all the ones who study. All the men and women who know a little better what the words of Scripture mean. They help us understand.

We have the ways and words of Christ and those who study him. They study what his words have meant and what they mean today. They keep on showing Christ.

The search for truth is hard, and it is good to have our Christ. Not to lose him now. To know his ways when we look for truth and search for what we need. To look with a question and walk with Christ, walk with his Spirit now.

What does Aunt Natalie think of truth?

She's very glad to have it and spreads it all around.
None of us is safe.

A Couple of Different Ways

What are the ways of Christ?

Seeing things in place.

Saying truth will honor man and man should honor
truth. Knowing truth should speak for peace and truth
should speak for justice and truth should speak for love.
One at a time or all at once, truth should speak for these.

Saying man should have his things, simple things and
more. That people have need of food and all good things
to drink and something warm to wear. Something good
enough for you and good enough for me. Saying man
should have the things he needs and man should have his
God.

This is one of the ways of Christ. Seeing things in
place.

What are the other ways of Christ?

Making things happen. Feeding the hungry and heal-
ing the sick and teaching us to pray.

Getting people together and keeping them unafraid.
Giving them heart to do their work. Telling his people
to go and do and get the good things done.

Does Aunt Natalie know what's good?

She knows what's good for her and she knows what's good for me. She never hesitates to tell.

War?

Why do people have wars?

We seem to let them happen. After hundreds and hundreds of years and even after that. It seems we let them come.

We spend great sums on war. We spend our money on soldiers and the things that soldiers use. We spend our money on soldiers and we make our soldiers fight.

We spend too little on peace, the study and keeping of peace. It seems that we are slow, it is hard for us to learn. The tools of peace are near but we are slow to take them up.

If I study about peace will that guy stop hitting me?

Yes, if you can get him to study with you.

What are the tools of peace?

As simple as something to share. Man has things his people want but man is slow to share.

Whatever people need, their freedom and their land. These are the tools of peace. Whatever people fight for.

Freedom and food and land. What everyone could have if man would share his world.

But man is slow to learn and he has reasons for his wars. He has goodness in his heart but he has other things besides. He has fear and he has greed. He looks around for strength to cover up his fear and he looks for wealth and power to satisfy his greed.

He learns to take away. He seems more fond of taking and keeping things away than learning when to give. Also he has pride. He has pride and many reasons and along with all his reasons it seems he wants to fight.

Man is slow to learn. Taking things away instead of letting people be. Letting people have their freedom. Letting people have their land. Letting people be. Man has many reasons and all of them are worrisome but some of them are worse. And so the battles come and many go along, saying they are right and praying God they are.

Does everybody fight?

No. Some say war is only right at times. Others say it never is, that war is never right and we should look for other ways. That war itself is a cause of war. That war won't solve our problems and killing calls for something that man should never do.

Maybe they are right. Maybe war is always wrong. These are questions we should think about. Questions we should answer when we think about our wars.

Her Again

If Aunt Natalie is so special how come she never mentions God?

She says he's not a good idea and we only waste our time. All the time we have, she says, and all the love we have, we need for one another.

If people don't believe in God, why do we care?

We like our people to think of him. We like our people to think of God and man together. We think it good for man.

We think it good for man to know that what he wants is God. His wish, his dream, his hopes, the best of what he wants is there with God.

We think it good for man to know he looks for blessed things. To know his search is right, to know his search is holy, having faith in what he wants. Every man and every woman, having faith in what they want, every child reaching out.

We think it good for man to know exactly what he is and what it is he reaches for. That man is man and God is God and man is a favorite child of God. That God is what there is. That God is what there is for man. And God forgive us slowly if we settle now for less.

Are we finished with that?

Yes, in a way.

Good, now I can hit him back.

Who?

My little brother. Who did you think I was talking about? The one that always hits me.

Church

Why do we go to church?

It's part of the way we live. One more thing to do in this world we see around us.

But why do we go?

To celebrate our God. The God we touch when we are touching one another. A reason why we touch and often touch with love.

To celebrate our God and give him thanks. Knowing God's own touch is real and that he touches every one of us and thanking him for that. And reaching for a friend so we can touch him back.

To celebrate our God in strange and holy ways. Like taking bread that he has blessed, and sharing it with others, and saying it is Christ we share.

To honor God who honors us. The Father, and the Son, and the Spirit with us now. To honor God and tell

Church

him things. What we can do for him and he can do for us. To ask his blessing on the world.

And for reasons of our own. And reasons saintly people have.

To bless the wonder in our lives.

Does everyone go to church? Everyone who thinks of God?

No.

Why?

There are many reasons. Maybe the Church has many things to learn about herself, and many things to learn about the world, and many things to do for man before she can offer herself to more.

Which means that we have things to do now. Things to learn about ourselves, and things to learn about the world, and things to do for man.

For the Church is you and I. The Church is you and I and everyone she comes to. Asking each of us to follow Christ. To follow God and follow man. To do the things the world wants, to do the things of God.

Reaching for what is true and doing what is fair. Reaching for those who wait. And she comes to bless us now. Asking each of us to try. Calling you and me and everyone we know. Asking us to reach now. As far as we can reach. Asking us to reach and touch the farthest child.

Why all the reaching and touching and all?

We like to get the exercise. It helps us reach some more.

Who is the farthest child?

The farthest away from the things he needs. Farthest away from the helpful things. Farthest away from the promising things.

The tired and the sick. The hungry and the cold. The lonely, too. Someone we forget. Someone overlooked. Someone put aside.

One or two or three years old. Seven or seventy-nine. Older than that, they are getting on and ought to be thinking of God.

The farthest child is anyone, anyone who waits. One, especially a child, one who waits for one of us. A child who will not run, a child who comes to stay. Anyone who looks around will find him waiting there.

The Church Is a Scourge

Does the Church always make us feel good?

No. She's a blessing and a scourge.

What's a scourge?

Anything that troubles us. It might have happened

yesterday and now again today. Anything that troubles us and never goes away.

Then why do we care about the Church.

She often helps us think of God.

She often helps us pray.

She calls to us as Christ has called, imitating Christ. She is keeper of his word, reminding us of Christ while he is gone. She calls to us and many people come, quickly or slowly, her reluctant and her saints.

She brings the day alive with God. She brings the day alive and God is with the hour, where God is always new, only dimly, warmly past, when God is now and man is now and both have things to do.

She is Christ once more, Christ again for all of us, imitating Christ, bringing grace for each of us, her sacraments are there. Her sacraments are there for each of us to share. To share with saints and saintly people. To raise ourselves with saints and ask for God.

Is Aunt Natalie a scourge?

Yes, the kind we like to have around.

Why is the Church a scourge though?

Because she's there, she's always there. Never leaving me alone and always after me. Always holding up her Christ to me and telling me to be like him. At times I know I can't, but she's always there reminding me to try, that Christ has said I can.

At other times I only see her people, not her Christ.

Someone's in my way. I know it isn't you, but if it were,
I'd ask you please to stand aside. Move aside and let me
find the goodness. I know that it is there. The goodness
and the promise and the person of her Christ. She seems
to hide him now.

No matter, I will find him. I know that he is there.
Tomorrow she will show him once again. She is a blessing like we say she is, a blessing and a scourge.

Sacraments and Such

What's a sacrament? Do we have any in the house?

Things like Baptism. Things like Holy Communion.
Things the Church will do for us when God is what we
want. When we find our God attractive and want to
bring him close. Ways that Christ has shown to us. Ways
that Christ has liked.

*If God is so attractive, why doesn't Aunt Natalie want
him?*

She is hardly what we call a true believer. She decided
very young that God was just a story and her thinking
hasn't changed. She is charming, she is gracious, and her
thinking hasn't changed since she was very young. She
was six, as I remember, six or eight, or maybe even four.

What's Baptism like?

A very special welcome for a very special person, any

child of God. A time for every single one us, for each of us is that, a child of God.

Those at a baptism are the parents, godparents, perhaps some friends and relatives, a minister or priest and the person to be baptized, usually a child. The child is often just a baby and, with any luck at all, the baby is asleep. A favorite time for people to say, this is a child of peace and joy, this is the one who will love.

The priest or minister asks certain questions and the godparents answer for the child. The questions have to do with whether or not the child wants his God, whether or not he wants to be a Christian. These are questions that will come again. The child grows and the questions stay. Is there a God I want? Is there a Christ I know? Is the Spirit at my side?

Those around the child will pray together and when the moment has arrived, the priest or minister says the words of baptism. I baptize you, you whose name I say.

I baptize you in the name of God, Father, Son and Spirit.

Or words that mean the same.

At the same time, he pours a little water on the child's forehead to show that this is a child of God, a child who is new. New and fresh and clean and all its sins come later.

With the pouring of the water, the child is formally a Christian, the newest one of all. With the pouring of the water and the saying of the words, God is with the child. The Spirit with a child, a child with his God.

Was Aunt Natalie ever baptized?

She isn't saying. We think she comes closest when washing her hair. As close as she cares to get.

What is Holy Communion? Does it get us wet like Baptism?

Communion is a time for doing what we want if what we want is Christ. A time to do what Christ has asked. A time for bread, to swallow bread, or swallow bread and wine.

To perform a simple act for a single reason, Christ. For the only reason, Christ.

To do what he has shown us. To do what he showed us many years ago. The night before he died, he took bread and blessed it and gave it to his friends. His friends were the apostles. He asked them to eat the bread and said it was his body. His friends were quite surprised and they wondered what he meant and they did what he had asked.

Then he did the same with wine. He blessed the wine and gave it to his friends and asked his friends to drink it. He said it was his blood. Again they were surprised and they did what he had asked.

That was the first Communion. Something new and strange and holy. Something new had come. He gave them bread, he gave them life, and life is what he offers us. Life of Jesus, life of Christ, a life to share with him and to nourish with his bread.

Walking to his altar, asking there for Christ, to say of

him in many different ways, something you have been is
what I want to be, something that you are is what I want.
Of all things else, this I know, what I want is good.

Christ is waiting. Christ is there. Christ is there for us
to take. A private thought or prayer is all we need to
bring.

Why did Christ use bread instead of something else?

Bread was probably in season.

No. Bread is important to many of us, just as Christ
can be. Bread of life, himself.

What about the wine?

Wine is important to some of us too.

Those Ministers and Priests

*What is a minister or priest? Someone who scares us a
little?*

Extraordinary people. When we like them, we call
them men of God, and when we like them less, we call
them other things.

They have the hardest job of all. They must speak of
peace to soldiers and talk of God to saints. Or speak again
of love or speak again of hope, where love has come and
gone, where hope has never been.

To scholars they must speak of truth or scholars turn

away. They must speak of truth to all of us, a hundred minds to reach, a hundred hearts to please.

Ministers do many things. Priests do many things. Some of what they do is different, some is much the same. What they do is done for God and you, for God and man, for us, and for themselves.

Some of what they do they do in church. Some they do outside of church. They look in likely places to see where God should be.

They look in likely places and bring him here and there. Bring him now where sickness is, asking God to stay, or bring him here when you are sad, asking you to smile.

Priests and ministers, how can they bring God?

God quickly goes along with ministers and priests. He travels very well.

God will walk with each of us, he surely walks with them. They give their lives to God, at least they try, and we think it only right that God should be with them. So God will come along with his ministers and priests each time they come to bless us, or pray with us, or touch our hand, or be with us in ways that Christ was with his friends.

All those priests and ministers. Is God with them more than someone else?

A minister won't think so and neither will a priest. They only know what we know. That all of us should care about our world. For caring makes our God come out and caring keeps him here, and which of all the ministers and which of all the priests will say he cares a little more than either you or I?

God has time for each of us so keep him out of corners and out from underneath. Let him take his place with you. That's all that ministers have done. And so it is with priests.

What would Aunt Natalie do if a priest came to see her?

She only talks to ministers.

What would she do if a minister came to see her?

She only talks to priests.

What would she really do?

She would simply be herself. Very friendly, sir. The way she'd be with someone who just dropped in from Mars.

A Child Is Ready

What is Confirmation?

At Confirmation, a child is ready to speak for himself, to say for himself he chooses God and wants him in his life. He is willing, anyway, to give his God a try.

Between the time he is baptized and the time he is

confirmed, a child learns many things about his religion, many things about his Church. If the Church has taught and the child has learned, the child might say that what he sees is good. That the Church he knows is good for him and brings him close to God.

In Baptism, the godparents speak for the child, in Confirmation he speaks for himself. The Church has chosen you and you have chosen her. The Church will know that what you choose is God.

The priest or minister performing the service, usually a bishop, asks that the Holy Spirit be with the child. He asks the Spirit to stay with the child, to keep, to teach, to bring him truth, to walk the world with him, to help him live as best he can the things that he believes, to watch the child grow.

At Confirmation, it's good to remember that the Spirit has his reasons, that his work is in this world, that his work is with the child, the one we see confirmed. And the world will be better the more they work together, that child and his God.

The Saints and Me

What are saints like?

All of us are saints or maybe should be, since God is with us now and God has touched us all. But some of us are special, a better kind of saint, and all of these it seems are different from myself. All the ones I know are truly good. People notice differences between the saints and me.

They live a different life. They do what we have dreamed.

The truth we want they seem to have. A truth they live, it helps them love, it seems they always do. A wondrous, often wordless, always certain truth.

They are different from ourselves, closer to our God than most. They seem to care the way that Christ has cared. It seems they always love, knowing better than ourselves that God has made this world, that we are here because of love, that love is why we're here. They keep repeating that, they go on repeating Christ.

What good are saints?

They teach us things. They show us Christ was right. That we can love our God and love our neighbors as ourselves. Not as well, perhaps, as saints, but well enough so friends will know that we are truly friends and God will know we think of him today.

Some of the saints we know about were martyrs. A martyr dies. He dies for special reasons, love of country, love of God, love of something he believes.

The church has many martyrs. People were afraid and didn't understand when the martyrs spoke of Christ, when they told of different ways and talked about their God.

Some of our martyrs are women, some of them are men. They died for love of God and hoped that some of us would see they also died for us.

Courage was a common thing with them, another act
of love. That is how we think of them, knowing they
have loved, knowing each of us can love.

Lots and Lots of Churches

Why do we have so many different churches? Aunt
Natalie says there's one for every different fairy tale.

Aunt Natalie should stay in shallow water. Others
swim, but she can only wade, though she really wades
quite well.

She's right about our numbers. We have many different churches, there are many of us here.

Baptists, Lutherans, Catholics. Methodists, and more.
Presbyterians and on. On and on for quite a while, on
and on to God.

People start to listen, people listen for their God. Everyone has listened, there is much to understand. To understand the Father, to understand the Son, to understand
the Spirit, find the Goodness in the land.

Those who listen get ideas, ideas filled with hope, listening to Christ, ideas filled with joy, hearing what he
said, ideas filled with love, doing what he asked. One idea
grew, it soon became a Church. Others did the same.

That is partly what our Churches are. Churches are
ideas, people with ideas, people with their prayers hoping God is in their midst. We say he is.

It's not surprising we have churches, many different

churches, there are many different ways to honor God and ask for him. The one for you and me is a matter for our conscience. A matter for our conscience, a question here of taste. A taste we have for Christ.

A Conscience and a Song

What is a conscience?

A feeling we have, a sixth or seventh sense. A feeling we're doing what's right, a feeling we're doing what's wrong. It helps us choose between the two. Our conscience isn't always right. We might discover later it was wrong. Nonetheless, it's nice to have. It keeps us good for days and days and sometimes even more.

Conscience is a blessing and a bother both at once. It looks inside our hearts and numbers all our sins, and opens all our doors, thinking truth might wander in.

Conscience is a friend. It tells me right from wrong. It helps me do what's best, so wish my conscience well.

Does Aunt Natalie have a conscience?

Hers is extra special. No one has to tell her what is right. No one has to tell her what is wrong. So far as we can tell, no one ever has.

Do we mean all these things we say about Aunt Natalie?

A Conscience and a Song

No. She is twice as good as me and half as good as you. Christ says we should love her. Many people do.

Why do we sing in Church?

Singing is a form of prayer, a common form of worship, a way we worship God. Lots of people singing, maybe two or three are good, maybe two or three know how. We hope they sing much louder than the rest.

God forgives our singing. He would tell us if he could that he forgives us many things. That he forgives us when we sing if we keep our voices down and let the ones who sing the best sing loudest, he would say.

God enjoys our singing. He knows what we have sung. That our song is one of hope, that we often sing of gladness, that singing can be fun. He would tell us if he could to go ahead and sing, to sing our song with others, that he likes his people close, to go ahead and sing and share the gladness he can bring.

We Worship

What does worship mean?

Some things are better than others. What's very good, we like. What's best of all, we worship.

If God is best for us, if God is what we say, we have ways to worship him. To show him what we want, that we have chosen him. With thanks to give and things to say, that we have chosen him.

We bring ourselves to him, and that is worship. We come with others to his church. To pray, to sing, to sit or kneel with those who feel the same, each of us with private thoughts, but worshipping together.

Every prayer and every song, each of these is worship. Every service, every mass. All the ways we honor him, the ways we worship God.

What's religion?

The things we've been saying. A way to live with people. With yourself and someone else. With people and their God. A way that brings us closer to them both.

What's the first thing to learn about religion?

Learn to be with people first. Every child does and every child is right. Learn what people are. If we can't tell what people are, how can we tell what religion ought to be?

How does worship help us?

It shows we have an interest. It shows that we can love. An interest in the world and how it works. In the world and its people.

We go to God in worship, we go and ask his blessing, on you, on me, on everyone we know, on that one over there. We ask his blessing on the world, that the one who made the world will make it work a little better, that the one who made the world will help us do its work.

It shows we care about ourselves and we care for others too.

So we go to him in worship, knowing God will send his blessing, for you, for me, and that one over there.

Who is that one over there?

Never saw her before. I thought she came with you.

What's a blessing, something good?

Yes, but God's is even better, God's is best. He blesses us with life, he gives us life. And he blesses us with grace so we can love what he has given. He gives us life and grace to make it good.

Grace and More Worship

All this grace, what is it?

Grace is one more reason for our church. Every prayer and every song, every sacrament and saint. Our services, the mass and every sacred rite. They bring us grace, the grace of God, the blessing that we ask. When God is close to us and we are close to him, when God has sent the Spirit and the Spirit being with us is the grace we speak about. The help he brings in being there. The hand of God on one of us. The hand of God on you.

Grace that finds itself in saints and works in ordinary women and ordinary men, the Spirit with his people, the Spirit with us now.

Grace of God, Spirit in our hearts and minds, Spirit at our side, the grace our people need when we look for better things. When now and then we feel there might be need for change.

Does Aunt Natalie have grace?

Yes. One of God's most noble acts. He blesses her in many ways. She doesn't seem to mind.

What's a mass?

A mass is one good thank you to our God for Christ his son, our Lord. Giving thanks for Christ.

A mass recalls the time of Christ just before he died. It speaks in prayer about his death and resurrection, his promises of life.

It recalls the first communion. The blessing of the bread and wine, the offering of these to God who is our father.

Near the end of mass, those who wish will share this offering, the offering that Christ had said was now indeed his body. The sharing of the bread, or bread and wine.

The mass is very old. It has always been a way of worshipping together, a way to offer thanks, a way to worship God and ask his blessing on the world.

Prayers and Sermons and Nuns Pray Too

The prayers I have to say. Why do I say them?

Prayer is the hope we have, the thanks we feel, the sadness we have at things. Prayer is telling these to God.

In private or together, with ourselves or other people, at home, in church or anywhere, when one of us will pray, with hopes to share and sadness, or thanks to give to God.

Prayer reminds us we have things to do. A world waits for us and God is waiting too. We know this when we pray. It reminds us people care about themselves, reminding us we also care, and tells us very quietly that we will let them know.

I am different when I pray. I am always something better. I am kingly like a king. I am welcome like a child. My prayer, like theirs, is special. My prayer, like theirs, is just for God.

When I have things I want to share. When I have hopes to share or sadness, or thanks to offer him.

What if Aunt Natalie changed her mind and prayed?

Then the Spirit could go home, saying to himself how well he'd done his work and all of heaven would ask if what they heard was real.

Why do we have sermons?

A time to sit and listen, something for ourselves.

The things we do in church are mostly done for God. We have prayers for him and music and sacred ways to honor him that Christ has said are good. What we do we do for God, except, of course, the sermon. He doesn't need a sermon. The sermon is for us.

The Church is partly sacred, having things to do with God, and partly only us. He comes to us in sacred ways, the rest is up to us and the sermon tries to tell us that, telling us of things to do when God is at our side. A way to act with God and man so those we meet will know it's good, having God around.

Sermons often speak of Christ, telling us his words. Telling us of Christ so we can recognize him now when we look at one another. To know him in ourselves and learn to see him in another.

There are many different sermons. They teach, explain and help us understand. They speak of hope, of looking all around. Often they will tell us what we should tell ourselves, to look a little farther and do a little more, to look around for Christ and do what he has asked.

Sermons may be short or long and mostly they will tell us that God is here expecting things of us.

What are nuns about?

Nuns, like ministers and priests, listen closely to their God and they like to answer him by doing things for us.

They laugh and sing like all the rest. They read a book or write a poem and go about their business which is teaching in a school, helping with the sick, working with the poor, or working in a distant land, wherever Christ should be.

They seem to say the best that they can do is follow Christ. Some will even close themselves away and pray for you and me, as Christ has done at times, or pray for grace themselves, as anyone would do.

Nuns have much to pray for, just as you and I. That God will bless their work, whether helping you and me or working with his people in a distant different land.

Do nuns ever get to heaven?

You will see them there.

Who doesn't get to heaven?

All the scaredy cats. All of us who run when we're faced with something good. God would never put us where we're most afraid to be.

Rules and Words

What are the Ten Commandments for?

The commandments are for all of us. They prove what we suspect, that God has thought about his people. They remind us of important things and let us know that God has understood us well.

He sees we look for goodness, he sees we ask for love and he says quite plain and simply that God is what we want.

He tells us not to be surprised. That we should listen to our hearts in our search for what is good and not to be surprised if our search will lead to him.

His commandments tell us more. I am better than before when I learn to love my neighbor. We should honor one another. I will ask for what is mine and not for what is yours. The world has things for each of us and certainly it's true that the best of what I find I keep for you.

Ours is not to harm, the commandments clearly say, we will try to do no harm. We will help each other grow, we will grow in love and grace.

These are things we know ourselves, these are things we want. The commandments say that we are right, that God has said indeed we are and tells us most emphatically to keep these things in mind.

Does Aunt Natalie keep the commandments?

Yes. Her favorite is the one that tells her not to bother with the rest. To choose the ones she likes and let it go at that.

Is that really a commandment?

No. But we won't tell her that. People learn to humor her and let her have her way. Those who love her like to live in peace.

Why do we say so many amens?

Amen is one of our better words, very popular in church. It is suitable and short, with many helpful meanings, two of which are *certainly* and *yes.* Meaning yes, of course I do, I have a question now and then, but yes I do believe, amen, I'm glad I do. Something I have heard is good. Something here I like.

It's the ending for a prayer. It's a prayer itself, no need for other words. Amen in all our churches to a God who gives us things, to a God who gives us life. Amen for you and me.

Some of The Things Are Amazing

Does the Church work miracles?

Only God works miracles. The Father, Son and Spirit. Miracles are always done by God. You and I do many

Some of The Things Are Amazing

things but God does many more.

He gives us life, as we have said. The life he gives us here is natural and good and we say we understand. It's a miracle, it's not. It is something we expect, and we think we understand.

But now and then we don't. Something different happens. Something more than natural, something more than good.

The deaf can hear, a child has life again, the dead are not so dead. Things that were are changed and all of us are puzzled, all of us are pleased. The storm is quickly gone, the water calm and things are what we wish for, what we want.

The Bible says that Christ did many things like this, that Christ worked many different miracles, that Christ was truly God. It isn't just the miracles, it's Christ himself who shows that he was God. How he lived and what he said, how he loved and what he did, the things he means to each of us, the way he died for man. All of this and more. The Father who called him Son and each of us who calls him Lord and God.

The Church has many people, many of them holy. None of them work miracles yet miracles are done. Miracles because of them—these, our saints, these, our holy people. God, it seems, has favored them and works with them in very special ways. A miracle because of saints, but always done by him. Never magic, only God, all the miracles are his.

God will work with each of us. No miracles for you, perhaps, nor maybe even me, but many things to do.

What does Aunt Natalie think of miracles?

She finds them most amazing. She thinks that everything's amazing and most of all herself. More of us should be that way.

Church and Faith and Why Can't We Sin?

What's the Church really? Only people with ideas?

The Church is all of us who look for God and show we look for him by looking all together. You and I and ministers and priests and nuns where nuns may be. The church is all of these and sacraments and saints and every form of worship that follows after Christ. All the people here who study what he said, all of us who know that Christ was God and man, with words for us to hear and ways of doing what is right.

The Church is all of us together and the Spirit in the middle or somewhere on the edge, protecting her from me and sometimes from herself. Telling her that Christ is true and all the truth around him will now or later come, to look with faith and heart and mind and know that he is with her, the Spirit with her always, just as Christ has said. The Church is all of us together and the Spirit in a special way, more with all of us together than with one of us alone. Doing things together seems to help.

The Church is even more. In a different way of speaking, the Church is everyone we know, everyone who ever honored Christ by seeing good in others and doing what is right. Maybe some have never heard of him, never heard of Christ, but still they do his work.

We like to think they're with us. That these who never think of Christ but often do his work are with us in the Church.

Aunt Natalie too?

Aunt Natalie too. But please don't tell. She would smile and scheme and maybe cast a spell. Each of us would pay.

What is faith? Something everybody has?

Faith is when my heart and mind agree that I am right. Sometimes mostly heart and sometimes mostly mind. Something's good and right and true. Somewhere here inside of me the things I love and all the things I know have come together now and they tell me God is real and I am right to want him close. Things are properly in place.

Faith is something I believe. A confidence I have, a confidence, a trust. Faith in you and faith in me, faith in this and that, faith in you and faith in God. Faith is just enough at times to keep things looking right, little enough at times to make me wish for more and little enough for some to make them look for other things.

Faith is yours and mine. We're not sure why we have

it, but the things we know and love can make us glad we do.

Why can't we sin? Why does the Church tell us not to?

She says that we shouldn't but knows that we will. It seems she loves us dearly, she knows that we'll be bad but she wants us anyway. The reason that she does is that she knows we're mostly good and says the good should be together now and then.

She knows that one of us will sin. That one of us will lie, that one of us will take what isn't ours to take, that one of us will harm another, needlessly will harm a stranger or a friend. She says that we have sinned when we haven't tried to love, if we hide ourselves from others and hide away from God.

She says that sin is just the opposite of love, the opposite of everything we want. That none of us would sin if we knew the harm it does—to you and me and the world in which we live.

If we happen to sin, what does the Church do?

She tells us we are right. Right to feel sorry. Right to feel wrong.

She knows what we are thinking. The harm we do, we do not like. The one we harm will like it even less, and Christ, who likes us most, will like it least of all. She says that we should come to him.

Come to him, she says, and ask forgiveness now. Make peace with anyone we've hurt. Make peace with those we should and always with ourselves and always Christ. She says that he forgives us and gives us each her blessing to show that this is so. She gives us absolution, forgiveness for a sin.

What's the biggest sin?

Not to be afraid of sin.

Absolution. Does it hurt?

No. It only helps. Done in the name of the Father. Done in the name of the Son. Done in the name of the Spirit. Forgiveness for a sin.

The Church is imitating Christ and doing what he said. That is what the Church is for. If I fail now and then, the Church is willing to forgive and do what Christ has said to her. Whose sins you shall forgive, they are forgiven, and those you don't, they aren't. Forgiveness for a sin. Given freely. Given often. Giving grace. Done in the name of the Father, done in the name of the Son and done in the name of the Spirit, God forgiving me.

Why should God forgive us?

Someone said he loves us.

Are we always forgiven?

Yes, if we repent. Which means that we are sorry, we wish what we had done were something else instead. We do not choose what's wrong.

And God forgives more quickly when we ourselves forgive. When we ourselves forgive what others do to us.

Anyone who harms us, anyone who sins against ourselves.

Forgiving shows we understand. It shows we know what sin is all about. That anyone can sin and not myself alone.

Even you could sin. I see it in your face, in the corner of your eye, but I forgive you now if you will do the same for me.

Let's All Go

How often should we go to Church?

As often as we please. As often as she likes us to, our Church. As often as we want him close, our God. For Christ will come along. He says he's always there when we gather in his name.

Once a week seems fair enough to some. The Church will let us know, she's the one who offers Christ.

We also go on special days, days the Church has set aside. Christmas, Easter, special days for Christ, blessed days for Christ and us.

Often we will go only thinking that we should. Other times we go because we love and look for things. We love and have desire and we look for what we want. And we bring ourselves with others to show we've chosen him.

Are you done with that?

Yes.

Good. But that was close. I think Aunt Natalie is coming.

The Son

Is Christ the one named Jesus?

Yes. Christ is the one named Jesus.

Christ is the Son, and like the Father and the Spirit, he is called God. That is what we mean by the Trinity of God. Where one and one and one is always one. Three different persons but the one same God. Father, Son and Spirit, but the one same God.

And the Son lived on earth for more than thirty years, where he was born to Mary and Joseph in the town of Bethlehem, and his parents named him Jesus.

And he could leap tall buildings as a child, but chose just to work and play and get the chicken pox instead. More like the other children of Nazareth would do. The place where Jesus lived.

Is all of that true?

No. There were no tall buildings in Nazareth, and Christ was a child like each of us. With friends and thoughts that children have, and things that children do.

And we do say he was God.

And it does seem right that God should come to the world. To grow as a child does and be with his people for a while. That Christ should come to quiet us.

For man is sometimes anxious with his God, and if he thinks of heaven, his thoughts are sometimes filled with fancy. And if he thinks of hell at all, he may laugh or cry or shake his head and walk away.

Quiet us? How does Christ quiet us?

In a way that works for everyone. By showing us his love. Another way, perhaps, is just in being what he was, in being God and being man, and showing us a likeness. Showing us that man in his moments is something like his God. That when man does reach for truth and what is fair for others, he reaches close to God. And when he reaches out for peace. And when he loves.

And this is both a comfort and a care. For each of us can do these things. Or some of them. Or one. And if we can't, Christ will do them for us. That's what he was doing on the cross.

Christ died for us?

Yes. We each have our way of doing things, and that was his way of doing things for us. His way of doing things the world wants, doing the things of God. His way of doing things for us when we do other things instead. Things that keep us small.

Like reaching out for something instead of something

else. When we close our hearts and our minds. When we keep ourselves away from one another and hide what love can bring.

For these are the things called sin. The common kind of sin. Keeping things away from man. Holding back from God by keeping things away from man.

And we think of Christ. Christ with his cross. Christ who died for each of us so the world might have what the world needs, and man can have his God.

And because of Christ, and strangely, and sometimes taking long, the world is more like the world should be, and God is pleased with man. A man or a woman discovers a truth and all of the people are glad.

And we know that there are other sins. Sins for only some of us. Like knowing Christ has done this and holding back our prayers. A private kind of sin. Keeping things away from God.

But Christ didn't stay dead, did he?

No. What we call the Resurrection. He was up and around in three days time, or back with us at least, and that's the loudest call for heaven that we have.

A call for those who need. A call for those who dream. That whatever is missing will come. That all good things will be.

Which sounds like another fairy tale.

Except that some of us do need things, and all of us have dreams. And the need is real and the dreams go on, and Christ did live with us and talk with us, and Christ did speak of heaven. And he understands our hearts, and has promises to keep.

Heaven Talk and Hell

What is heaven anyway? What are heaven and hell?

A place to be and a place to be away from. Which isn't exactly true.

For heaven is not a place. It is neither up, nor down, nor sideways. It follows us around.

It is something we will feel, something we will have. Having peace and having life. To be with love and beauty always, having life and love and truth. Things we say that God is.

Things that were, even before the first man raised his head and wondered. Things that are, and were, and will be. With or without a world. With or without a universe to search through.

And if someone mentions hell, it is sometimes best to laugh or cry, or shake our heads and walk away. For hell is hard to imagine. If there really is a hell, maybe its like knowing something very good is close. And not being able to reach. Or not wanting to. Or just not feeling up to it. That would be hell, but at least a person could live with it.

Which doesn't answer the questions well. For these

are things that God knows, and our own thoughts fill with fancy.

And if we wish for angels, maybe there are angels, but devils we can do without.

If we took all the bad there is in the world, though, and put it all together in a single place, and gave it the shape of a man, and a tail and hooves and devil's horns, and an ugly face and a name, we could call it Satan. For that's what God called evil.

And if we think of evil here, if we think of the bad there is, we can think of the blindness of man. Where man doesn't see the harm he can do. Doesn't see, or doesn't care to. When he doesn't understand and doesn't try.

Where the blindness of man is our reason for prayer, and the reason we reach for truth. Hoping man will find his way. Leaving things like evil and sin. Leaving our Satan behind.

Do angels have wings?

Only the older models do. Those I've seen lately look a little more like you.

Christ at Twelve

How do we know about Christ?

The Bible tells of Christ. The Bible and the Church. The Bible has two main parts. The Old Testament that tells of God and creation and the Children of Israel, and the New Testament which tells of Christ. The story of Jesus and what he did and said.

The story of Jesus is told in the Bible by his friends—his disciples or apostles. They were the ones who knew him as a man. The ones who followed him and taught what he had told them and knew that he was God. That Christ, a child of Bethlehem, was then and even now the Son of God.

It says in the New Testament, the part we call the Gospels, that Christ was quite a child. When he was twelve he did a thing that most of us would never understand, or do ourselves at twelve or any other time.

He disappeared for several days and when his parents finally found him, he was sitting in a temple talking to some elders, teachers who were older, much older than himself.

He told them things they didn't know. He answered all their questions and seemed to have more answers than they had questions for. They wondered who this child could be and how did all the answers come when he was only twelve.

He had talked with them of God who was his Father. He told them what it was the Father wanted, when all at once his other father came. His father who was Joseph and his mother who was Mary and both of them were cross, of course, but glad that they had found him.

He told them why he'd gone. He said he had to do the Father's work, to do the work of God. A good and holy reason, a good excuse at that, a son of God has many things to do.

Then Jesus went back to Nazareth with Mary and Joseph. He went with them as any child would, for he was theirs to have and keep, just as you are his. So far as we are told, that's the only time he stayed away from them.

Was Jesus right or wrong to disappear?

Who knows? Sometimes no one else can judge us. We have to judge ourselves.

Names and Christ and Children

If his name is Jesus, why do we call him Christ?

Use either one you wish. His name is Jesus, and Christ is what he does. Christ means savior or deliverer, both of which are helpful. So use the name you like. Aunt Natalie can look the other way.

When Jesus was a man, did he still like children?

His disciples weren't too sure at first. A group of people gathered, listening to Jesus, listening to Christ, and some of them brought children. When they took the children to Christ, the disciples tried to stop them, thinking Christ should not be bothered, but Christ said otherwise.

Christ said yes I want them, bring your children here.

Bring the ones I like the best, bring each of them to me.

Look at them, he said. Look upon them closely. Be open like a child. Stand before your God as little children would, knowing you are his.

Christ was fond of children and most of us believe that he was right.

A Special Way of Talking

Did Jesus make speeches?

Sermons, they were called, and often filled with parables.

A parable is a kind of word picture, a story with a meaning and another meaning too. A picture made with words, but seen a different way it's made with different words instead.

Probably the best known sermon of Jesus is the Sermon on the Mount . . . .

Wait a minute. Why did he go to a mountain?

Why not? It's good to get out of the house now and then.

What did he say on the mountain?

He had parables to tell. Stories he told so the people there could learn and other words as well that sounded much like this.

Blessed are the poor for they shall be in heaven.

A Special Way of Talking

And blessed are the meek—those who never reach for everything in sight. Theirs is heaven, too. (Jesus said earth—the meek shall inherit the earth—but seen a different way, the word he used was heaven.)

And all the clean of heart—those of us who sin the least.

And all the ones who look for peace and all the ones who bring it.

And everyone of us who isn't treated fairly and everyone who suffers just for doing what is right.

Heaven is for all of these, he said.

Is that a good sermon?

Yes. It says to many the best is yet to come and it tells us more besides. It tells us to be more like God. Not to be outdone. Do right here what God himself has promised. Do it here and now. Heaven should have to wait.

Feed the hungry all around us. Bring comfort to the sad. Honor those who sin the least, be one of them ourselves. Think how good the earth would be if heaven had to wait.

Why did Jesus talk in parables?

People like their parables. Everyone likes a story.

And Jesus might have said to himself, it's best I only show the way, not take you by the hand. It's best you find the truth yourself.

And might have said besides, those of you who want it already have the truth. Look into your hearts.

The Father

If the earth is our mother, does that mean the sun is our father?

Maybe so. The sun is big and beautiful like fathers are. And sometimes seen too little and sometimes seen too much. And it's full of bluster and warms the earth to give us life. A likely father.

Isn't God a better father?

Now we go slowly, for things are different here. There are things to look for, and words that we grow up to. Things that all the world wants.

A love for truth. A love for justice. What is true and what is fair. Where truth can bring its many things and every child can share.

And a love for all things living, except for maybe those crawly things. And a special love for man.

If God helps us feel this way, we should choose him. For this is what we ask of him. This is what we want. And peace for a moment. And joy. And wonder . . . all the time.

Truth can bring us things? I thought that God brought everything.

God has many helpers. Truth is one of them.

Is God angry if we don't choose him?

Probably wistful and maybe downright sad. But God

knows he is hard to find, and he has a different heart. So if he sees that we don't choose him, he simply chooses us. And each of us, ready or not, and some of us dragging our feet, becomes a child of God. He is father to us all.

Aunt Natalie, too. Is she a child of God?

Aunt Natalie, too. And listen to her scream.

Do we know much about God?

No. God is the Creator and we are part of his creation. But we are new at this. We are the only things created that ever asked why, and our answers touch the lives of men. So we should be curious, but careful. We will let them smile at our questions, but neither God nor man should have to weep at our answers.

Doesn't God tell us about himself?

Nothing loud and clear. And that does seem atrocious. Not as loud as we would like and not as clear.

The Bible, though, tells about God. It was written many years ago, and many of us believe God helped the men who wrote it. The Bible has strength and beauty and anger and joy and comfort.

It tells about God, and the patriarchs of Israel, and the people of Israel, who were called the chosen people of God. They were chosen by God to keep his word and they do this even today.

But it seems good to read the Bible in the company of teachers, or at least with a watchful eye. For God is not a simple God, and the Bible has many stories that seem so strange to us, and here and there some things to say that go a thousand ways.

Perhaps, as with children, God tells best by showing us his work. His world, his people and the universe around us. And we can say God's work is good, and God is therefore good, and certainly he loves us for giving us these things.

And how we act before God. How we love him back. How we care for the things he gives us, and how we share with others. And the smallest prayer we thank him with, or say to him in sadness, or say to him with hope. These seem more important than what we know about him. Or think we know. Or what we are likely to believe.

The World Again

Did God create the world?

Yes.

How big is our world, really?

It changes all the time. As different as our people. A billion different people and several billion more. It changes with the years, it changes with the day.

Look and see it now. What we have and what we do is all the world there is, what I see and what I wish, what I know about and feel. My world is what is brought to me and all the things I find, and yours is much the same.

You are pleased at times and sad. Your world is big and

small. Your world is always better or not as good as mine. There are times when you would change with me and I would change with you. Our world is sour-sweet, our world is good and bad. Something in our world is good and something could be better.

Our world is much too small if something can't be better, our world is much too small for us when everything is here, when I have nothing more to want, if I have tasted something good and I have nothing more to ask.

Our world is small again when things are much too far, when everything is far away and everything I want is out of reach.

If what I want is over there and I am over here, my world is small indeed. If it takes away my wishes and takes away my hope. If it doesn't bring the things I need and keep them over here.

My world will be big enough. My world will be bittersweet and big enough for me. With things to have and things to want and room enough to look. A world should have promise, a world should be big. A world for you and me.

Big like a building? Or big like the land?

Big like growing, big like growing up. Getting used to things and reaching now and then.

A world for every one of us, letting people live and giving people room. Room enough for hope. With much to have and much to want, and reason to expect that what they want may come.

Letting people find their pleasure and follow after dreams. Giving people reason to know that God is good, giving people reason for expecting much of him.

To make a world big we must start with certain things, certain necessary things. Give a people food, give a people freedom, give a people time. Give a people time to look around and reach. Give a people time to reach for him.

Adam and Eve and Us

Who were Adam and Eve?

Adam and Eve is a story in the Bible. According to the story, Eve was the very first woman and Adam was the very first man. They lived in a place called Eden and they were very happy indeed. It seems they had no friends but they were happy even so.

There wasn't any hunger there. There wasn't any sickness. There was no pain in Eden. They had everything to live for and little fear of dying, no such thing as death. They were pleased with God and God was pleased with them.

But then the trouble came. Adam and Eve both did something wrong and both were sent away. God banished them from Eden. He said that they should leave and learn of other places and learn of other ways. To go where pain and sickness are. To learn about the hunger and learn about the pain.

What does the story mean to me?

The story has many meanings. That suffering is with us for a while. It can't be wished away. That suffering is here, not to run from it, but learn. To understand the hunger, to understand the pain. To find the one who suffers and find how we can help. And if it bothers us to help, then we should welcome those who will. We should welcome those who do.

The story tells us sin is most important. Most importantly wrong. It seems to make things worse.

For all of us are wrong when we close our hearts and minds, shutting out the light, closing out the good, keeping God away. Adding to the suffering, adding to the pain.

It tells us each of us is Adam and each of us is Eve. The wrong we do is never ours alone. It has a way of touching man.

For man is not yet perfect, he has no Eden here. He has no Eden now but it will come. What he wants will come through Christ.

Christ who suffered too. Christ who knows the ways of man. Christ who is our promise, the things that we can be.

If Christ is bringing us something, what do we do till he gets here?

Do whatever you have to and be whatever you should. Be and think and run and jump and now and then if things are right perhaps get something done. With luck, we might at that.

Never wait for Eden. Heaven is another thing, what we have is here. A world with its joy, a world with its pain, a world with things to do and ways for us to help.

Knowing the Spirit is here. Knowing he has reasons, that God and man have things to do together.

To know his reasons are good, better than standing around. That life is a matter of growing, of thinking things, and doing things, growing up to God.

Isn't it spooky to have the Spirit around?

It's nice to know he's here. It's nice to know he helps. Life would be spookier without him.

Growing

How do we grow up to God?

The words are not too wise, we should look for better words. Something we can't do, growing up to God. Something we can only start.

If we knew what growing meant, it would help a little here.

Maybe part of it is joy. Maybe joy is part of growing and the Spirit brings it out. Joy at what he show us, joy at what we find. Things that make us happy and turn our hearts to God. Maybe joy is part of growing and the Spirit makes us glad.

Maybe growing is to suffer, but how can that be so, for

growth is something good and suffering is pain. Yet suffering is here. It is something people do and something Christ has done. Anyone who suffers and anyone who cares. Anyone who says it shouldn't be. Maybe suffering and pain are part of growing.

Maybe truth is part of growing too. To look around for reasons, to look for better ways, to understand ourselves, to understand our world. Maybe truth is part of growing and the Spirit helps us see.

Maybe peace and justice count. What Christ has said we need, saying those who ask for peace and those who ask for justice are asking things that everyone should ask. Maybe peace and justice count.

Maybe love is part of growing. Love that looks beyond ourselves to see the people there. Sees the need for peace. Sees the need for justice. Sees the need for truth.

Maybe these and more are all a part of growing. That the love we have for someone and the ways we try to help are part of growing up to God, but only part.

The rest is up to Christ. The difference is with him. Maybe that's why he will come, maybe that's why we believe that Christ will come again.

What will he do?

Bring us all together. Bringing all of man together, bringing man to God.

Having put aside the cross, having put aside the ways of man, when Christ is only God.

To put aside the cross, to bring us even closer, bring us all the way to God.

With ways and reasons we don't understand. A single act of God, a simple act of will, of wanting it that way. When the Spirit has finished his work, when Christ has come for us, when God has willed that man should be with him.

Does God ever celebrate and sing?

Only on your birthday.

Does he ever feel foolish?

Only on mine.

Other Things Too

What do we think of death? What do we think when people are gone?

We think about their life and we think about their silence. Someone waits for Christ. Something started, something done, something waited for will come. A very quiet wait. A very quiet, silent, sacred wait. This one waits for Christ.

What about little children? Do children have to wait?

Saints and little children. Maybe these don't have to wait. Children aren't good waiters, they don't wait well at all, and a saint would never be without his God. Maybe Christ will understand this. Maybe saints and little children are never asked to wait.

Who do we meet in heaven?

Only the best people.

What about the others?

He hasn't told me yet. When he does, he might surprise. He might leave it up to you. He will leave it up to you and let you go and find them. He will let you find the good, he will let you find the bad. He will let you find the one of us who isn't touched with either, he will let you find the one of us who isn't touched with both. You might have trouble then. The one of us you're looking for might be hard to find.

One thing sure, each of us will know. We'll know if we are good like you, we'll know if we are not. A time will come for finding out and each of us will know. A moment with our God. To see with God the good we've done, to see with God the harm.

Maybe happiness is knowing. A moment with our God, seeing clearly once. Maybe pain is knowing too.

The moment could have beauty, the moment could be long, the moment will be long enough for each of us to know.

Will she be there?

Aunt Natalie? Yes, Aunt Natalie will. And you can count on that. She wouldn't miss it for the world. She doesn't miss a thing.

Other Things Too